Gary Wilmot's

BIG BOOK
OF
PRACTICAL
JOKES

Gary Wilmot's
BIG BOOK
OF
PRACTICAL
JOKES

 Robson Books

First published in Great Britain in 1989 by Robson Books Ltd,
Bolsover House, 5-6 Clipstone Street, London WIP 7EB

British Library Cataloguing in Publication Data

Wilmot,

Gary, 1954 -

Big book of practical jokes.

1 . practical jokes

I . Title

790.1'3

ISBN 0 86051 609 1

Typeset by The Picador Group, Bristol

Printed in Great Britain by St Edmundsbury Press,
Bury St Edmunds, Suffolk.

CONTENTS

INTRODUCTION

I've always been a bit of a practical joker. I can still remember the time I got sent out of the classroom for leaving a spider on the teacher's chair, and the look on my father's face when he discovered I'd sewn up his pyjamas and he couldn't get into them. I soon learned that it is OK to play practical jokes on some people, but definitely not on others. This still applies, and now that I am older and wiser I realise it's no use playing tricks which involve spilling water in the living room and ruining the carpet, or the kind which might amuse young people but are likely to give some older ones a terrible fright. So my advice is — go carefully.

That said, you can still have a great deal of fun. There are over 150 jokes in this book, suitable for all kinds of people and all kinds of occasions, but especially appropriate, of course, for April Fool's Day. I have divided them into four sections: Old Favourites — those we all played as children, and which our parents probably practised, too; Planned Pranks, which require a bit of forethought, preparation and props, though nothing that can't easily be found in the average household; Very Silly Jokes, for people who don't mind making fools of themselves; Theatrical Tricks, for those who relish a bit of drama; and Quickies, instant tricks that can be performed on the spur of the moment. Just to show I'm not the only joker around, I have included some genuine jokes that people have played over the years, and pretty amazing they are, too.

Turn the pages of this book very carefully. Between two of them you will find a nice, crisp, new £5 note. Have fun!

OLD FAVOURITES

Classic tricks
that have been
played for generations

SHUT THAT DOOR!

Equipment: a yard or two of string

This trick requires two doors that are close together. Two bedroom doors side by side on the landing would be ideal, especially if both rooms contain unsuspecting victims. Simply tie the string to both door handles, leaving it fairly slack, and knock on both doors at the same time. One occupant is bound to open the door first, but as soon as the second door is opened, the first will slam shut! Open it again and the second door will close with a bang! This could carry on for quite a while before the two people realise what has happened.

APPLE PIE BED

Equipment: a bed with sheets on it

This classic has been played for many years. Traditionally it needed a bed made up with sheets and blankets, but it can be done with a bed that uses a duvet as long as there is a top sheet as well.

For either kind of bed, remove the top sheet, loosen the bottom sheet at the foot of the bed, and bring it back up to the top of the bed, folding it neatly over the blankets or duvet so that it looks like the top sheet. The bed will now appear to be perfectly normal, but on getting in, the victim's feet will only go down a few inches.

LOOK UP

Equipment: none

This is a very old trick, but it never fails to work. It is best played in a busy place, with plenty of people around. We used to play it in the classroom.

Whether indoors or outdoors, simply look up and stare at the sky or ceiling. If a friend is near by, touch him or her on the shoulder and point upwards. Before you know it, people will be craning their necks to look up — mystified as to what you have seen.

MAKE HASTE!

Equipment: none

This is an excellent April Fool's Day trick, especially in a large household where everyone has to get up and rush out in the morning. Secretly alter every clock in the house so that it is exactly one hour fast. Don't draw anyone's attention to the time, which will arouse suspicion, but wait until someone notices the kitchen clock. The chances are that he or she will be surprised, and go into another room to check the clock there. Amazingly, it will tell exactly the same time. With luck, you will very quickly start a full-scale panic! To be really sneaky, play this trick the week before the clocks go forward in spring.

You: 'Did you get wet before you got to school/the office this morning?'
Friend: 'No.'
You: 'I thought not. You can always tell when someone hasn't washed.'

DAFT DRAWERS

Equipment: a chest of drawers

Still in the bedroom, here's another trick to play on an unsuspecting guest, or member of the family. Remove each drawer from the chest one by one, carefully empty out all the contents of each and put them away for safe keeping, and then replace the drawers *upside down*. In the morning, when the room's occupant goes to get out clean underwear, he or she will be totally baffled.

BIG FEET

Equipment: sheets of newspaper

If you want to tease someone about his big feet, roll up some sheets of old newspaper into balls and stuff it into the toes of both shoes. Obviously the shoes won't fit properly, and the owner will struggle, assuming either that his feet have grown or that the shoes have shrunk. The victim will be totally bewildered if you don't cram in too much newspaper, but just a little, which can't easily be felt or seen.

EGG YOLK

Equipment: empty eggshells

Offer, as a special treat, to cook breakfast one morning for the family. Lay the table carefully, put out the cereals, fruit juices, marmalade, and so on, and prepare plates and eggcups for each member of the family. Boil a pan of water and then, when the eggs are all sitting in their cups, call the family down to breakfast. They will tuck in eagerly — only to find that their 'eggs' are empty shells! For you will have saved the shells for a few days, cleaned them carefully and put them upside-down in the cups, so as to look exactly like whole eggs. You can even drop the shells beforehand into hot water so that they feel warm and indistinguishable from the real thing.

TEA-HEE!

Equipment: a teapot

This trick can be played alongside the egg joke, or separately. Announce that you are going to make a nice, strong, hot cup of tea. Put out the milk and sugar, the cups and spoons, and go into the kitchen to boil the kettle. When you return, pour out the tea and hand round the cups, warning everyone not to burn themselves as the tea is very hot. They will carefully pick up the cups and take a sip, only to look very surprised — for the tea will have been made with cold water! You can do the same trick with coffee and a coffee pot.

KICKING AGAINST THE PRICKS

Equipment: several prickly hairbrushes

This joke can be played on its own, or combined with Apple Pie Bed. Just put one or more prickly hairbrushes into someone's bed, far enough down for them to be out of sight when the bedclothes are turned back, but in such a position that your victim's feet will come into contact with them as he pushes down into bed. He will think he has crawled into a nest of hedgehogs — an impression you can reinforce by pre-bedtime talk of how many hedgehogs visit your garden at night, how tame they are, and so on.

ROUND THE BEND

Equipment: a long measuring tape

This is the kind of prank that university students used to get up to during Rag Week. All you need is a street corner and a couple of gullible passers-by.

Go out into the street and find a likely corner. When someone comes along, you pose as a surveyor, and say you have to measure the building on the corner. Remark that you are waiting for a colleague who hasn't turned up, and invite assistance. Ask the passer-by kindly to hold the end of the tape for a few moments, while you go round the corner and measure the other wall. Once out of sight, you seize on another likely victim, and repeat your story, with a slight difference. This time your colleague is holding the other end of the tape and *you* have to rush off to make an urgent phone call, or whatever. You then leave both unfortunate people holding the tape, and slope off to a vantage point from which you can see them but they can't see you. After a while, one of them will wander round the corner, looking decidedly puzzled. If you are worried about losing your measuring tape, use a long piece of string instead.

CRAZY SHOPPING

Equipment: a crazy shopping list (see illustration)

If someone kindly offers to go to the shops and asks whether you want anything, request a few items that you have jotted down on a list. Hand over the prepared list, folded over so that he or she doesn't read it immediately. On reaching the shops, your friend will have to hunt for a place that sells boiled potatoes and sheep's eggs. The list will soon be revealed as a spoof — but it should provide a good laugh.

WEIGHING HEAVILY

Equipment: bathroom scales, a metal ruler

You have to be a bit careful about whom you choose to play this trick on, for it might upset some people. The victim should be someone who is rather weight conscious. Simply alter the dial on the scales so that they record a heavier — or lighter — weight, depending on the effect desired. Assuming, however, it is a heavyweight you are trying to fool, you can add to the fun — even if you do reveal yourself as the joker — by holding a metal ruler over the edge of a table or windowsill as your victim steps on the scales, and hitting the end of it with your other hand. It will make a lovely 'booiinnnggg' sound, which, combined with the few stones already gained, will convince him or her that the scales have broken.

BLOOD BATH

Equipment: red food colouring, or red ink

Next time someone in the family watches a particularly frightening film on television, offer to soothe his or her nerves by preparing a bedtime cup of cocoa and running a good hot bath. The cocoa (which should be made properly) will alleviate any suspicions your kind offer may have aroused. Run the bath, and pour in a few drops of red food colouring or red ink. Call out to your victim that everything is ready — and then hide out of sight. You will soon have the pleasure of hearing a piercing scream, at the sight of what appears to be a bath full of blood!

You: 'Did you know they're not going to grow rhubarb any longer?'

Friend: 'No. Why?'

You: 'It's long enough already!'

KISS ME QUICK

Equipment: a prepared notice and piece of sticky tape

This is one of the oldest jokes in the book, but it's still fun to play at a party. Prepare a notice. It might say, 'Kiss me quick', 'Give us a wink', 'Pat me on the back,' 'I'm an idiot' — or any other statement that might be particularly appropriate to the person concerned. Attach a piece of sticky tape to the notice, and, while an accomplice distracts your victim, stick it on his or her back, pretending to be showing affection, removing a stray hair, or whatever. It can sometimes take quite a long time before victims of this joke realise why people insist on patting them, winking at them, or giving them a smacker on the cheek.

ON THE WAGON

Equipment: blackcurrant juice, cold tea, liver salts

Here's a way of persuading boozers to cut down their alcohol consumption. The trick takes a while to prepare, however, for you have to save the empty bottles of their favourite tipple. Then you make up fake drinks. Gin and vodka, being colourless, are the easiest; you can just fill the empty bottles with ordinary tap water. Whisky or brandy can be faked by using cold tea — but make sure there are no leaves in it! You can experiment with different strengths of tea in order to get the right colour. Brandy is darker than whisky, so you may need a stronger brew. White wine or vermouth can be faked by using a quarter of a bottle of cold tea, topped up with water; and red wine by using blackcurrant juice, possibly diluted slightly, depending on the wine in question. Of course, it is very difficult to fake the foil on the neck of a wine bottle, so reserve the wine trick for part bottles, if any are left around. And don't forget the liver salts. They're for the tonic to go with the gin. Fill an old tonic-water bottle three-quarters full of tap water and add a teaspoonful of liver salts. Screw the top on tightly, and when it is undone it will fizz just like the real thing. But the taste — disgusting!

THE RIGHT STAMP

Equipment: none

Try this trick on a friend. Say, 'Do you collect stamps?' If they answer, 'Yes,' then say: 'Well, here's one for your collection!' and stamp on his foot! If the victim replies 'No,' then say: 'Well, here's one to start you off!'

Don't stamp hard, or you might lose a friend.

ENTER AT YOUR PERIL

Equipment: a cushion

This again is a very old joke, though anyone with any sense will play it with a lightweight cushion rather than the traditional bag of flour.

Leave a door slightly ajar and balance a cushion on top of it. Then, as you and your victim approach the door, stand back and politely let him go through first. As he pushes open the door, the cushion will fall, and hit him on the head.

THE WHEEL THING

Equipment: none

This is a very old joke, ideal for playing on children with their first bike. Let them get going on it for a while, and then point to the bike's front wheel and shout, 'Hey! Did you know your front wheel was touching the ground?' Or point to the back wheel and say, 'Hey! Did you know your back wheel was going round?' It will take them a while to realise that this is what is *supposed* to be happening!

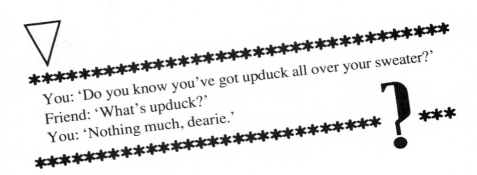

You: 'Do you know you've got upduck all over your sweater?'
Friend: 'What's upduck?'
You: 'Nothing much, dearie.'

PRESENT PRANK

Equipment: wrapping paper

Next time you buy your nearest and dearest a smallish present, wrap it up so that it appears to be big. This is easy if a birthday occurs shortly after Christmas, because you can hoard all the old wrapping paper. But you can always use tissue paper, or even newspaper, as long as it hasn't been round the fish and chips. Cardboard boxes help, too. Imagine a pair of ear-rings wrapped up to look like a television set!

APPLE SLICED

Equipment: an apple, a needle and thread

This is a truly amazing trick. Your victim will pick up an apple, take a bite, and the fruit will fall apart!

Thread the needle with strong thread or cotton, and push it through one side of the apple. Bring the needle and thread out of the fruit, then push it in again and along a second side of the apple. Bring the needle out and push it in once more, along the third side of the fruit. You should by this time have travelled all the way round the apple. Pull gently on the two ends of the thread, and you will slice right through the fruit's centre. Remove the thread and give the apple to your victim to eat. After a bite or two it will simply fall apart in his or her hands. Don't prepare the apple too soon before the trick is played, or it will go brown.

SWEET DREAMS

Equipment: various, see below

If anyone you know tends to fall asleep on the sofa after Sunday lunch, or at any other time, there are a number of tricks you can play on him.

Make a sign out of cardboard saying 'Original Sleeping Beauty', or 'Quiet, Man at Work Thinking', or 'Do Not Disturb, Growing Roots'. Prop this up beside the sleeper — who may well awake to the giggles of anyone near by.

If the victim sleeps heavily and is not easy to wake, put a dunce's cap, or some other silly hat, on his head. If he wears glasses, very gently stick little shapes on them, so that when he awakes he'll see hearts or stars and be very puzzled.

And with the co-operation of other people in the house, you could concoct an elaborate trick to convince the victim that he has been asleep for hours. Set the clock several hours ahead, draw the curtains, and switch on a light so that it looks as if it is evening. You could even leave a cup of cold tea beside the sleeper, and, as a final touch, get other people to put on their dressing-gowns and sit in the room with cups of cocoa as if they were on their way to bed.

PYJAMA PRANK

Equipment: pyjamas, or nightdress, needle and thread

With a needle and thread, loosely sew together the legs and arms of a pair of pyjamas, or the sleeves or armholes of a nightdress. Then wait for a shriek at bedtime as the victim struggles to get into night attire! Take care not to make the stitches too tight, or the material may tear.

SWEET TOOTH SWITCH

!

Equipment: liver salts

If someone eats too much sugar, here's a trick which might put him off for life. Empty out the sugar bowl, and fill it with liver salts instead. They look quite similar, and when your victim reaches for the bowl he is unlikely to examine it too closely. He will spoon several helpings into his tea or coffee — and then blink in amazement, for the drink will begin to froth and foam, and may even overflow into the saucer.

BLOTTING YOUR COPY BOOK

Equipment: paper or blotting paper and a bottle of ink; scissors

Even in these days of ballpoint pens, some people still use ink and fountain pens; and anyone who does is liable to make blots. Make some spoof blots of your own for April Fool's Day by splattering ink on to paper or blotting paper, leaving it to dry. Then cut carefully with scissors round the blots and place them individually where they are likely to cause the greatest consternation. On the white tablecloth set for tea? In somebody's homework exercise book? On a photograph of Aunt Ida? There are all sorts of wonderful possibilities.

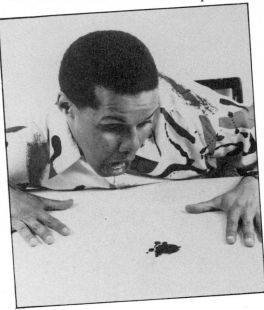

BUN FIGHT

Equipment: iced buns, an un-iced bun, a tube of toothpaste

Put the iced buns on a plate, and then get to work on the un-iced bun. Squeeze toothpaste on top of it in a pattern to match the iced buns. If they have a cherry on the top, put one on top of the spoof bun, too. It should look exactly the same as the others.

Then offer your victim a bun, having arranged the plate so that the spoof bun is likely to be the one taken. Eat a bun yourself, so there is nothing to arouse suspicion. But when the poor victim takes a bite — ugh!

HOT SANDWICH

Equipment: a sandwich, plus chilli, paprika, strong mustard, etc.

This is another sneaky food trick. Offer to make someone a sandwich with his or her favourite filling — anything will do. Right in the middle of the sandwich put a patch of something very hot-tasting, like strong mustard, chilli, paprika, chopped ginger root, and so on. Your victim will bite happily into the sandwich for a mouthful or two until suddenly — help! Fire! If you are kindhearted, you will come to the rescue with a glass of water.

COLD COMFORT

Equipment: none

This is a similar trick to the Blood Bath on page 18. Again, offer to run someone a lovely, warm, relaxing bath. Set out towels, favourite soap, bath salts and so on, and tell your victim the bath is ready. Then hide! For he will be very cross indeed. Why? Because you will have filled the bath with cold water, that's why.

POLTERGEIST POWER

Equipment: invisible thread

Some shops sell very fine 'invisible' thread for mending. You can create all kinds of poltergeist-type effects with it. Tie it to someone's knife, fork or spoon at the table, leaving a long enough end to come over to you at the far side of the table, and hang over the edge. Give a gentle tweak, and the knife will start to move mysteriously across the table, apparently as a result of supernatural powers. Or attach the thread to the handle of an empty mug — with the same result. Make sure, however, that there is a clear path between you and the object you are trying to move, or you will cause a lot of upset.

The thread can also be tied across a doorway or passageway, but take care. The idea is to create puzzlement at this invisible resistance, not to trip someone up. Arrange the thread so it is at mid-calf or mid-thigh height, and don't attempt the trick at all if there are small children about, who would walk into it at face height.

32

WHO'S SPEAKING ?

Equipment: a telephone

You can have all kinds of fun with a telephone, whether you are making the call or answering it. If making a call to a friend, cover the mouthpiece with a handkerchief to disguise your voice slightly and pretend you are calling from Buckingham Palace about the hundredth birthday of Mr So-and-So, or from Number Ten Downing Street about Mrs ----'s letter to the Prime Minister. Say you are phoning from the Water Authority, warning everyone in the house not to run a tap or flush the loo for the next three hours, because of tests, or from the Gas

Board, threatening to cut off the supply if the bill isn't paid in the next two days. The possibilities are endless. You can also try putting on a foreign or regional accent, if you are good at these; or adopt a lisp by putting your tongue behind your lower front teeth when you speak.

When receiving a call, give the brisk answer, 'Waterloo Bridge'. This will totally flummox the caller, who will start by assuming it is the wrong number and end up realising that the bridge doesn't have a telephone. Or announce that you are George's Pig Farm and were they ringing about the boar, or the local council's Pest Officer, and that you'll be round directly about the fleas — whatever seems most appropriate for the caller. You can have a great time for a few minutes.

PLANNED PRANKS

Tricks that need
a bit of preparation

HAPPY BIRTHDAY!

Equipment: none

Although a birthday may not be the ideal time to play a practical joke, little harm can come from this one. It is best if you can gain the co-operation of other people in the house, and you all agree to pretend that you have forgotten the person's birthday. Get up early and collect all the cards that have arrived before the birthday girl or boy awakes, leaving just the boring post — like the gas bill — on the mat. Then, when he or she gets up, say nothing at all about the birthday, and carry on as if it were just an ordinary morning. If the victim begins to show signs of looking really unhappy, get everyone to cluster round and burst into a rousing chorus of 'Happy birthday', and hand over the cards and presents.

GLASS GAS

Equipment: a drinking glass, cling film

This trick can be played in two ways. You need a piece of cling film, to be stretched smoothly across the top of a drinking glass, and therefore exactly the same size, so as to be virtually invisible. You can use a glass which contains something to drink, or an empty glass into which someone is going to pour a drink. In the first instance, your victim will be very surprised not to be able to drink out of the glass; in the second case, if he or she tries to pour anything into the glass, it will spill all over the place. For this reason, it is best to play the trick with an ordinary tumbler, likely to be filled with water in the kitchen, rather than with a wine glass, which may spill wine all over the tablecloth.

SHRUNKEN HEAD

Equipment: a large cooking apple, a knife

Primitive tribes in certain parts of the world in times past used to practise cannibalism, and preserve and shrink the heads of their victims. These macabre souvenirs would turn up in the West as curios, often having been brought back by soldiers and explorers. You can make your own 'shrunken head', with which to frighten nervous people, out of a cooking apple.

Choose an apple that is more or less head-shaped, and carve features upon it — eyes, eyebrows, nostrils, a mouth and ears. Leave it in a warm place for a week or two, on the top of a boiler or in an airing cupboard, where it will shrivel and wrinkle realistically. When it has achieved the desired appearance, stick some crêpe hair or wool on the top to look like hair. Then, when Aunt Ethel comes to tea, ask her if she's ever seen the memento your great-grandfather brought back from Borneo — and display the head. Be ready to catch her when she faints.

TRAILING THREAD

Equipment: a needle and a reel of thread, a jacket

Does anyone you know have the irritating habit of pulling bits of thread off your clothes? If so, here's a good trick which might cure the habit. If possible, wear a jacket with an inside pocket. If you don't have one, a small polythene bag attached to the inside of your jacket with a safety pin will do. The idea is to thread the needle from the reel without breaking the thread, so that you have a thread many yards long. Drop the reel into your inside pocket (or into the polythene bag) and pass the needle through to the outside of your jacket; then remove the needle, leaving just an inch or so of thread showing. Sooner or later this sharp-eyed person will come along and say, 'Just a moment, I'll remove this thread from your coat', take hold of it and pull. The reel will then unwind, and unwind, especially if you start to walk off. But move away backwards, for the expression on your victim's face will be worth seeing.

MUG GAME

Equipment: a mug or cup with a broken handle, Blu-Tack

You know how easy it is to knock the handle off a mug, cup or jug — perhaps when washing up? Often the handle breaks off quite cleanly, leaving no nasty splintered edges. When this happens, stick the handle back on again with a couple of blobs of Blu-Tack and wait for a chance to play a trick with it. Pour in a little tea or coffee, and hand it to your victim on a saucer if it is a cup, or by the base if it is a mug. When he tries to pick it up by the handle, it will remain in his hand while the rest of the cup or mug will fall. Bear this in mind when preparing the trick — it may be as well to do it on the grass in the garden and just put water in the cup.

RINGING SPRINGS

Equipment: small bells

Pet shops sell little bells which are intended to be hung in budgerigars' cages or even for affixing to cats' collars. Next time you see them, buy half a dozen or so, for you can play a good trick with them.

Choose a victim whose bed has good old-fashioned springs, and attach the bells to them. Then, every time he or she turns over in bed, the bells will ring. Sweet dreams!

FINGER TIP

Equipment: a matchbox, some cotton wool, some red paint or ink, a handkerchief

A particularly gruesome trick can be played on an impressionable person with the above equipment. Tell him that a friend of yours had an awful accident while doing some carpentry or cutting up food in the kitchen, and sliced off his finger. Remark that he has saved the finger in the hope that it can be sewn back on again, but has given it to you to put in the fridge until tomorrow. And, of course, you just happen to have it in your pocket. 'Would you like to see it?' you ask.

The awful fascination will prove too much, and the answer, after some hesitation, will be 'yes'. You put your hand in your pocket, and bring out a matchbox, wrapped in a handkerchief. With your other hand you open the matchbox, to reveal a finger, packed in bloodstained cotton wool. To make it even more horrific, say that the finger is still alive, and as proof, get it to wiggle!

The finger is, of course, your own. Make a gap in the short side of the matchbox 'drawer', and cut a U-shaped, finger-sized slot in the sleeve that goes over the drawer. Stain the cotton wool red with paint or ink, then slip your finger into the matchbox and carefully pack the cotton wool around it, hiding the 'cut' end. If you hold the handkerchief round your hand so as partially to conceal it, you will find that the trick will work for long enough to cause momentary horror at the sight of the 'severed' finger.

ALARMING!

Equipment: several alarm clocks

Try this trick on anyone in the house who sleeps very heavily. Collect as many alarm clocks as you can — borrow them from your friends, if necessary — and set each of them to go off at five-minute intervals, finishing with the time at which the heavy sleeper would normally get up. Hide them in different places in the bedroom — under the bed, behind the chest of drawers, and so on. If this doesn't get the lazy so-and-so out of bed in time, nothing will!

SNEEZE TEASE

Equipment: a large paper or cotton handkerchief, a small, bouncy ball

Here's a good throwaway trick, which can be performed almost anywhere. You start to sneeze, 'Aaaaaarrrtishoo!', pull out your handkerchief, blow your nose on it, then throw away the hanky — and it bounces! Onlookers won't be able to believe their eyes.

The secret is to sew a small, bouncy ball into the centre of the handkerchief, or hold it in place with a small rubber band. If the hanky is large, you should be able to conceal the ball quite well. Then you pretend to blow your nose on another bit of the hanky so that it appears to be quite ordinary, before throwing it away. You may find that the ball doesn't bounce well on carpets, so choose a floor with a hard surface when you throw it away. And before you are accused of being a litter lout, pick it straight up again to prove otherwise.

You: 'What has six legs and jumped over the moon?'
Friend: 'I don't know. What has six legs and jumped over the moon?'
You: 'A cow.'
Friend: 'A *cow?*'
You: 'Yes. I added two legs to make it a bit harder.'

MONEY MAKING

Equipment: a £1 coin, an empty matchbox

If you get proficient at this trick, you might end up quite rich. Choose a gullible victim, and show him the empty matchbox and the £1 coin. Put the coin inside the box, and rattle it to prove the coin is inside. Then ask your victim to put another £1 coin in the box. The conversation then goes like this:

You: 'Two pounds is still quite a lot of money, isn't it?'

Victim: 'Yes.'

You: 'You could buy two or three magazines, eight or nine newspapers, a box of chocolates. Would *you* like to make some money?'

Victim: 'I certainly would.'

You: 'Well, there's £2 in this matchbox. Will you buy it from me for £1.50?'

Most probably your victim will take up the offer, and be pleased to have made 50p out of it, quite forgetting that one of the £1 coins in the box was his already!

LIGHT SUGAR

Equipment: polystyrene packaging foam

If you cut some polystyrene packaging material into small cubes the size of sugar lumps and hide them in a sugar basin among real lumps, you can play a nice little trick. When offering a visitor some tea, politely pass the sugar, and offer to put in the lumps yourself, so as not to reveal that they are lighter than real ones. The guest may not notice immediately that instead of dissolving into the tea, the lumps are floating on its surface, but the surprise will not long be delayed.

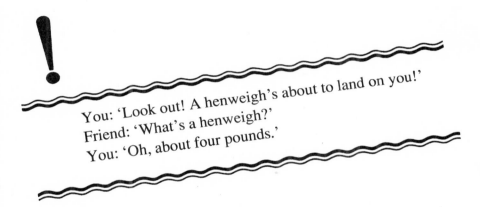

You: 'Look out! A henweigh's about to land on you!'
Friend: 'What's a henweigh?'
You: 'Oh, about four pounds.'

TELLY TRICK

Equipment: a tape or cassette recorder

If someone you know has a favourite, unmissable television programme, tape its theme music secretly and store it until you get a chance to play this trick. One day when the telly addict is distracted and busy, and may be less aware than usual of the time, play the theme music and shout, 'Hey, *Coronation Street/Neighbours/Dallas* has started! Come quickly!' The victim will charge into the living-room in a great tizz, only to discover that the music has stopped and you are quietly watching a completely different programme.

KEY TO THE PROBLEM

Equipment: some old door keys

A collection of old door keys can provide lots of fun. Clean them up a bit so they look like keys that are in everyday use, carry them in your pocket, then wait until you are walking home with a friend one day. Think of an excuse for the friend to hand over his or her door key; if weighed down with shopping, for example, you can offer to take the key and open the door with it. Slip it into your pocket, and swap it for one of your old keys. If it is a Yale key, substitute a similar one of your own, if a mortice key, then substitute your own. Toss the key in the air a few times, catching it neatly, then, just as you are approaching the house, toss it in the air again near a drain, and don't catch it, just let it fall down the drain. Your friend's face will be a picture. Profess to be terribly sorry, and suggest ways in which you might fish the key up out of the drain. Before your friend actually gets to the stage of rolling up a sleeve and fishing around in the dirty water, produce the real key from your pocket and admit it was just a joke.

UNEXPECTED SHOWER

Equipment: paper cups, a pin

Next time you are having a picnic, or a meal in the garden, with friends, prepare a few trick cups. Make a few holes with a pin near the top of several cups, and then partly fill them with lemonade — or some other drink. Just before your victim, or victims, starts to drink, offer to top up the cups, as you didn't put enough in before. As soon as the lemonade reaches the holes, it will start to spray out gently in a shower all over the drinker. The holes will be virtually invisible, so there will be considerable surprise.

SOCK SHOCK

Equipment: a needle and thread

Prepare a shock for someone by sewing the two sides of a pair of socks together just below the tops. Don't do it too tightly, or they may tear. Leave just enough room for the victim to start pushing his feet into the socks, but not enough for him to get then on, which will cause a great deal of puzzlement and surprise. It is not a good idea to try this trick with stockings or tights, however, for they will tear instantly.

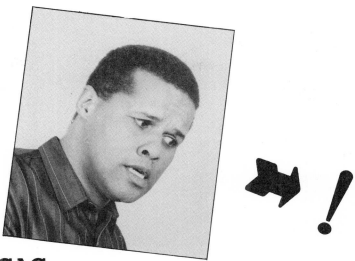

GHOST GAG

Equipment: a cassette or tape recorder

It's all very well dressing up in sheets and running along the corridor at night going 'Ooooooooooo', but people tend to discover who you are. A much better trick is to tape some ghostly noises and play them at a time when obviously you can have had nothing to do with them.

Take a tape that plays for an hour on one side, and run half of it before you start recording, so this first half is blank. On the second half, record some ghostly wailing, some slow, deliberate and echoing footsteps, the rattling of a heavy chain, the howling of wind in the chimney, an owl hooting, and so on. The time to play this tape is late at night, with the family or friends gathered round, and the subject of conversation steered around to the supernatural. You may, for example, have been watching an eerie film on television. Secretly set up the tape, bearing in mind that for the first half hour nothing will be heard. This is the great advantage of the prank, for if you are sitting around innocently when the noises start, not having moved from your seat for half an hour, you will not be suspected of being its perpetrator. You could even set up the joke and go out. When the noises start, don't be the first to draw attention to them, but when people do begin to notice, then join in the general scaremongering. You should have a lot of fun!

****

► You: 'Do you know something?'
Friend: 'No, what?'
You: 'You really are ignorant, aren't you?'

****

GRAVEL BED

Equipment: a handful or two of gravel, small pebbles, or dried peas or beans

Do you remember the story of the princess and the pea? The princess had such fine and delicate skin that she could feel a pea in her bed through several layers of thick mattresses. You can test the royal qualities of a friend without the mattresses, by just putting a few small pebbles or whatever under his or her bottom sheet. Put them a little way down so that they are not obvious the minute your victim pulls back the covers. There may be a lot of tossing and turning, and trying to smooth out the lumps in the sheet, before the cause of the trouble becomes evident. If the intended victim just goes to sleep without noticing anything, you must resign yourself to the fact that he or she doesn't have blue blood.

PERMANENT ICE

Equipment: some clear plastic, an ice-tray

Buy a small sheet of thick, clear plastic, and cut it into small cubes. Put these cubes in the ice-tray, fill it up with water and freeze it in the usual way.

When someone next wants an iced drink, get out your prepared ice-cubes. They will look just like ordinary cubes, but when their thin outer layer has melted, the rest will stay floating in the glass. It is a good trick to play on a really hot day.

SPUD U DON'T LIKE

Equipment: saucepan, sugar, water, apples, potatoes, cocktail sticks

Caramel is made by heating sugar and a small amount of water in a saucepan until it melts. Take care, however, for it becomes very hot and can cause a burn if it splashes you. Use it to coat well-scrubbed apples, into which cocktail sticks are stuck, to create classic toffee apples.

If anyone in the house is making toffee apples, or if you fancy making some yourself, make a few spoof ones too. Instead of apples, coat some apple-sized and *clean* potatoes with the caramel. Keep them separate from the real ones so that you know which are which, and then offer them to friends. When they take a hearty bite out of them, they will be *very* surprised. You'll probably have to give them a real one to cheer them up.

RICE SHOWER

Equipment: a friend's umbrella, some rice

You can play this trick with a single umbrella, or on a rainy day, when there are plenty around, with several. Simply pour some rice (uncooked, that is!) into a closed but unfurled umbrella — and wait. Sooner or later the umbrella's owner will pick it up, take it outside, open it up, and — hey presto — a shower of rice!

WATER SHOWER

Equipment: a plastic bottle, a pin

Use a pin to pierce a ring of holes in the bottom of an empty plastic bottle with a tightly fitting cap. Fill the bottle to the brim with water, and screw on the top tightly. Dry the outside of the bottle. While the lid is on, the bottle will not leak. Find a likely victim and tell him that you are having difficulty in unscrewing the cap and ask him to help you. As soon as the top is loosened, water will start to pour through the holes in the bottom of the bottle, wetting your poor victim's feet.

MIND READING

Equipment: a pen containing no ink

Tell a gullible friend that you have the power of reading what is in his mind if, unseen by you, he writes it down. Give him the pen without any ink (but of course don't tell him it is empty), a piece of paper, and somewhere to sit and write — say, in the far corner of the room. Tell him that as soon as he starts to write you will be able to 'read' it. He will, of course, be unable to write anything.

There are two ways of playing this trick. Either you can say, 'You haven't written anything, so I can't read your mind,' or you can wait until he tells you the pen won't write. You can then retort, 'Hmm, I always knew your mind was empty.'

READING ALOUD

Equipment: a prepared notice (see illustration)

Make a notice like the one pictured here, show it to a friend, and ask him to read it aloud. Unless he is very, very careful, he will say, 'A tree in the garden'. However, it doesn't say that, does it? (You could make some money here. Bet your victim he can't read your notice correctly — a bet he is bound to accept.) You could, of course, make a notice that reads, 'A fool in the the family'.

BLOWN OVER

Equipment: a large, heavy book, a polythene bag or a balloon

This trick can also win you money. Stand the large, heavy book on a table and bet someone he can't knock it over by using only his breath. He will huff and puff until he is purple in the face, but won't manage it. Then you can reveal how it is done. Put a polythene bag or a balloon underneath the book, and simply blow into it. As the bag or balloon inflates, the book will start to teeter until, finally, it falls over.

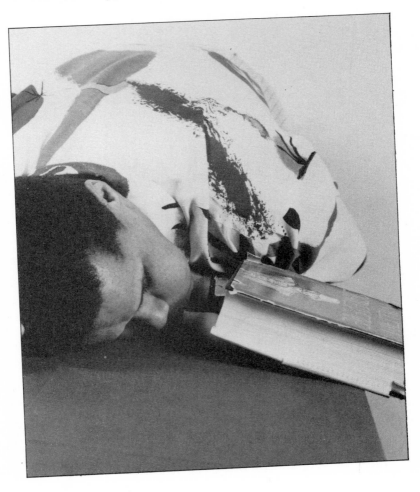

UNDER-WHERE?

Equipment: none

This is a great April Fool's Day joke. On the previous evening, make the rounds of the family's drawers and remove from them all clean socks and underwear. Check the airing cupboard, too, and take everything out as well. Hide all the stolen underwear somewhere in your own room — and wait for the frantic panic on the morning of 1 April when no one can find any clean underclothes.

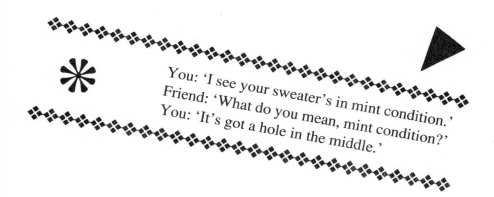

You: 'I see your sweater's in mint condition.'
Friend: 'What do you mean, mint condition?'
You: 'It's got a hole in the middle.'

HAT TRICK

Equipment: a hat, some talcum powder

This trick shouldn't be played on anyone likely to wear the hat soon for an important occasion. So if your victim is going to Ascot, or to a wedding or christening, give it a miss. But if the hat is just for pottering in the garden or keeping the rain off, then it's worth trying. Simply pour some talcum powder into the hat, and leave it upside down. Sooner or later the owner will put it on and get engulfed in a great pother of powder.

RIPPING YARN

Equipment: a piece of paper, or two strips of Velcro

At the exact moment someone in trousers bends down (perhaps to tie up his or her shoelaces), tear up a piece of paper and shout out, 'Oh dear! You've just ripped your trousers!' You will find some types of paper make a better sound than others — tracing and greaseproof papers are particularly good. A piece of Velcro also makes a good ripping sound when the two strips are pulled apart.

Since you may have to wait some time to catch anyone bending down in this way, an alternative is to bait the trap by placing a £1 coin in your victim's path. He or she will be sure to spot it, and bend down to pick it up.

TISSUE TROUBLE

Equipment: a box of paper tissues

Even the victim — in this case someone with a cold or suffering from hay fever — will get a laugh from this trick. Carefully pull the tissues out of their box and stick each one to its neighbour with a little blob of glue on either side. When the glue has dried, fold up the tissues carefully and pack them back in the box. When the unfortunate person feels a sneeze coming on and grabs a tissue, a whole string of them will come out of the box.

HOLE IN THE MIDDLE

Equipment: a plastic spoon, a hand drill

With the drill make a hole in the centre of the spoon at least one-tenth of an inch wide. Put the spoon in the sugar basin. When someone tries to take a spoonful of sugar, it will all run out of the hole, which will be hidden by the heaped-up sugar — until, of course, it has all run through.

COINING IT

Equipment: some coins, some glue, a piece of cardboard, a pair of scissors

This will fool any light-fingered person who may be tempted to pick up loose change that happens to be lying around. Spread a little glue on a piece of cardboard, and then stick a few coins on it. Put more glue on top of the coins, and stick more coins to them, then more glue and more coins, until you have quite a little pile stuck together. Don't pile the coins too neatly, they will look more realistic if they are a bit untidy. When all the glue has dried, cut carefully round the cardboard base so that it cannot be seen, and leave your pile of coins on the sideboard or the mantelpiece, where they will be visible and tempting. The would-be thief will be in for a surprise!

RING, RING!

Equipment: a telephone, a tape or cassette recorder

You can have a lot of fun by recording the sound of the phone ringing. Try to record it for quite a long time, and await your moment. If someone is expecting a particular call, wait until he or she is in the bath or the loo, and then play the recording. As your victim rushes to the phone, stop the recording; or simply leave it playing, so that it goes on ringing even when the receiver is picked up. Since there will be nobody to speak to at the other end, he or she will assume that there is something wrong with the phone, rather than suspect that the ring is on tape.

PILLOW TALK

Equipment: newspaper, aluminium foil

This trick takes a while to prepare, but it's worth it. Make lots of little balls from the newspaper and aluminium foil. Then remove someone's pillow from its pillowcase, and fill the pillowcase with the balls of paper and foil. Give yourself plenty of time — you'll need it. At bedtime your victim will settle down only to find sleep impossible, what with the lumps and bumps, and creaks and squeaks.

FORGED LETTERS

Equipment: a typewriter, headed writing paper if possible.

This amusing trick involves typing an official-looking letter, all the more convincing if you have a friend with access to a sheet of impressively headed writing paper. A letter from a firm of solicitors, for example, could inform your victim that Great Aunt Miranda has just died and left him or her half a million pounds. The possibilities are endless.

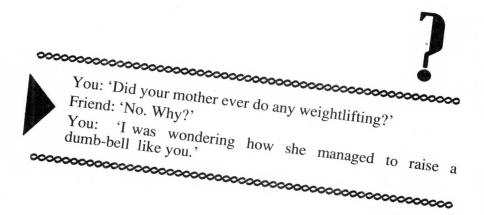

You: 'Did your mother ever do any weightlifting?'
Friend: 'No. Why?'
You: 'I was wondering how she managed to raise a dumb-bell like you.'

SMASHING TIME

Equipment: some broken crockery, a box, and wrapping paper

Next time someone in the house breaks a cup or a plate, or both, collect the bits. Put them in a small box, wrap the box in pretty wrapping paper, suitable for either a Christmas or birthday present, and await the appropriate occasion. Rush towards your friend, holding out the 'present', and pretend to trip and drop the box. There will be an awful crunch, and the recipient's face will drop. Apologise profusely, but then set matters right by producing the real present.

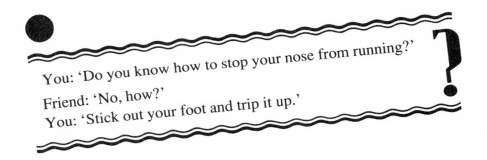

You: 'Do you know how to stop your nose from running?'

Friend: 'No, how?'

You: 'Stick out your foot and trip it up.'

GHOSTLY KNOCKING

Equipment: a small stick, a length of thread

Mysterious tapping outside a window at night could well upset someone of a nervous disposition — especially if there has been spooky talk before bedtime, or if you have tried out your ghostly tape trick (see p112). You can engineer a bit of haunting quite easily with a small twig and a length of thread. Tie the thread to the twig, suspend it outside the window, and tie the other end of the thread to the window catch. Make sure the curtains are drawn before your victim retires to bed. On anything but a very still night, the wind will blow the twig to and fro, so it will tap gently but persistently at the window.

BOOKSHELF BOTHER

Equipment: none

Here's a good long-term trick to play on someone who has lots of hardback books with dust jackets. Get the victim out of the room — you might even engineer a lengthy phone call — long enough to swap the dust jackets of the books, leaving the correct jackets, though not the correct books, in their accustomed places on the shelves. The next time your friend looks for *Roget's Thesaurus* and finds instead a book on potted plants, or a children's bumper joke book instead of the *Complete Works of Shakespeare*, he will be somewhat perplexed, to put it mildly. The sad thing is that you won't be there to see the continuing unravelling of your trick.

DON'T MOVE!

Equipment: a paper cup full of water, a broomstick, a chair

Here's a way of keeping somebody in one place for a very long time. Tell your chosen victim that you are going to show him a really amazing trick. Then carry the cup of water, broomstick and chair into a room in which the carpet doesn't matter too much. Climb on to the chair, position the cup against the ceiling, and the broomstick against the cup, to hold it in place. Then ask your friend to hold the cup in position with the stick for a moment while you get down from the chair. He is bound to agree, wondering what the amazing trick is going to be. Once he is holding the stick, get down from the chair, calmly carry it out of the room and don't go back! Your victim may well be there for ever!

LOOK, NO HANDS!

Equipment: a table covered with a cloth, a glass of water, a hat

Stand the glass of water on the tablecloth, put the hat over it and say, 'I bet you I can drink that glass of water without touching the hat.' Of course, your audience will not believe you. Lift up the tablecloth, crawl under the table and make slurping noises as if you were drinking the water. Then come out from under the table and say, 'I *told* you I could drink the water without touching the hat.' At this point, curiosity will overcome commonsense among your watchers, and someone is sure to lift up the hat to see if the water is still in the glass. At that point you grab the glass and drink the water. You have won your bet!

HANDCUFFED

Equipment: a heavy piece of furniture, such as a sideboard, table or grand piano

Bet your victim that you can clasp his hands together in such a way that he will not be able to get out of the room without unclasping them. He, of course, will not believe you, and will take on the bet. Lead him to the piece of furniture, place each of his hands on either side of, say, the table leg, and then clasp them together. He is now effectively handcuffed to the table, and most certainly will not be able to get out of the room without unclasping his hands.

NUT CASE

Equipment: some walnuts, a screwdriver, some glue, paper and crayons

Carefully prise open the shells of one or more walnuts and remove the kernels. Then put a surprise in their place. It might be a drawing of a funny face, a note reading 'Fooled ya!', a sweet, coin or button. Run a small amount of glue around the edge of each nut and stick the two halves of the shell back together again. If you do it carefully the nuts should not appear to have been tampered with at all. Put them back among other, ordinary nuts — and wait for the shout of surprise when someone tries to eat one!

You: 'What's black and white and red all over?'
Friend: 'I've heard that before. It's a newspaper.'
You: 'No it isn't. It's a panda with measles.'

LEAPING HAT

Equipment: a hat, two strong rubber bands, four safety pins

Slip the safety pins over both ends of each rubber band, and attach them to the sweat band of the hat, so that each rubber band is stretched across the inside of the hat.

When someone puts the hat on, it will shoot up in the air again. Or you can demonstrate the trick yourself, to make people laugh. Children, in particular, love it.

HARD CHOCOLATE

Equipment: a chocolate bar, a small block of wood

Take the wrapper off the chocolate bar very carefully and save it. Then cut a small block of wood into the same size as the bar or slightly smaller than it. Melt some of the chocolate in a saucepan over a low heat and pour it over the bar. When it has set, wrap the bar up in its paper again. Choose a friend who is particularly fond of chocolate, get it out casually, start to unwrap it and then thoughtfully invite him or her to take a bite first. Don't choose anyone with particularly weak teeth though, or they may send you their dental bills.

PEA SHOOTING

Equipment: some dried peas, some hot water, an empty carton or paper cup, a tin tray

This is another fiendish trick guaranteed to scare the wits out of anyone who's a bit nervous. Hide the tin tray, with the carton or cup full of dried peas on it, in your victim's bedroom — well out of sight, behind the dressing-table or under the bed.

Just before your victim goes to bed, pour some hot water on to the peas. This will cause them to expand and, as they do so, they will leap out of the carton and land, with a loud noise, on the tin tray. It may be worth trying out the trick first to see how long it takes before the peas start to jump.

CUTTING THE CORD

Equipment: a doorknob, a piece of string, a cup or mug, a pair of scissors

Tie the string round the handle of the cup or mug and attach the other end to the doorknob, as shown in the illustration. Then challenge someone to cut the string without letting the cup or mug fall, and without touching it.

Can it be done? Of course it can. Simply cut through the loop in the string. This way the knot will not be touched, and the cup or mug will not fall.

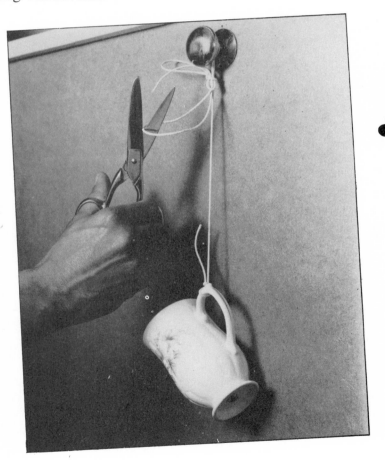

GIANT WASP

Equipment: a bag from a cereal packet, a fly

Trap a fly inside an empty bag from the inside of a cereal packet, and screw the top round so that it can't get out. Then tell a friend that you have caught the biggest wasp ever seen, which would sting him to pieces if it were released. Hold the bag near his ear. The fly buzzing around inside will sound like a giant wasp.

WHAT A CLANGER!

Equipment: a number of small metallic objects, such as keys, tin lids, scissors, cutlery, etc., plus a bag to put them in

This is a trick designed to fool anyone who habitually does the washing-up. Offer to help one day, especially on an occasion when the best plates or cups have been used. Run the water and start to wash up, then drop your bag of metal objects on the floor. Call out, 'Oh, no, that was one of the best plates/cups!' People will rush in alarmed, when you can have the pleasant task of reassuring them that it was all a joke and the plates are unharmed.

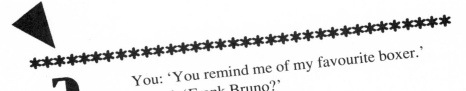

You: 'You remind me of my favourite boxer.'
Friend: 'Frank Bruno?'
You: 'No, he's called Rover.'

RATTLING GOOD TIME

Equipment: metal nuts, old keys, or a length of old chain, string

Collect together all the metallic bits and pieces and thread them on to a piece of string. If you are using a piece of chain, you can use the string to fasten its two ends together. Where? Around the bumper, the axle or the exhaust of someone's car. On being driven away, there will be a fearful noise, and the driver will be convinced that something dreadful has happened, and that the car is in urgent need of repair.

MAGIC CEREAL

Equipment: some Puffed Wheat, a plastic spoon

If you like Puffed Wheat for breakfast, try this trick in company before you pour any milk on to it. But it will only work if the atmosphere in your house is dry and warm.

Rub the plastic spoon hard on some woollen material, then hold it above your bowl of Puffed Wheat. If all goes well, the cereal will leap up into the air towards the spoon. You, of course, pretend it is magic cereal, which only obeys the commands you give it. If you keep the rubbing of the spoon secret, no one will know how you do the trick.

THE DAY'S NEWS

Equipment: two newspapers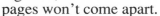

This trick is likely to make your victim very cross indeed, so it might be wise not to be around when the truth is revealed. Take the outside pages of today's newspaper, and wrap them round the inside pages of a newspaper that is at least a week old. Hide the outside of the old paper, and the inside of the new, and leave the trick paper lying around for someone to pick up and read. If you are brave enough to stay around, wait for a bellow of rage!

Another trick is to prepare a newspaper as described above and then glue all the inside pages (i.e. those of the old paper) together, so that when someone tries to read the paper, the pages won't come apart.

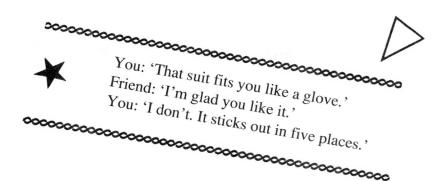

You: 'That suit fits you like a glove.'
Friend: 'I'm glad you like it.'
You: 'I don't. It sticks out in five places.'

LEAPING SNAKE

Equipment: a spring, or wire from which to make one, some green or brown material, a box, biscuit tin or jam-jar

The idea is to make a 'snake' which will leap out of its container when someone removes the lid. You need a spring which will compress right down, but you can easily make your own with some thickish but bendable wire. To do this, take a rod of the length you want the spring to be — for a small spring this could be a pencil, for a large one, a broomstick — hold the wire in place at one end of the rod, and then turn the rod, so that the wire twists in an even coil round it. Leave a bit of space between each coil of the wire, so that you can compress it into a small space. When it is long enough, cut the wire and slip the coil off the rod.

Then make a cover for the spring, long enough to cover its full length when it is not compressed. A green or brown material with a subtle pattern is best, and all you need do is sew it up into a tube. Add a couple of buttons for eyes, and a piece of red string for a tongue, if you want to be really clever.

Now compress your 'snake' and squash him down into a container with a tightly fitting lid, such as a tea caddy or a small screw-top jar. Then, when someone comes to open the tin or jar, the snake will leap out — to startling effect!

MONEY SOCK

Equipment: an old purse, or purse frame, a long sock

A purse frame is the metal part at the top of a purse with which it opens and closes. You can buy them at craft shops, or you could take one out of an old purse and use that. Attach the top of the sock to the frame, and roll up the sock so that it looks like an ordinary purse. If you carry it around like this with your money in it, and then unroll it in a shop or on the bus, feeling around in the toe of the sock for your money, you should get a lot of laughs.

GENUINE JAPES 1

PILTDOWN MAN

In 1912 science was a great deal less advanced than it is today. Scientists had for many years been seeking evidence of a link between the apes and the remains of the earliest known humans, and with the discovery of a fossilised skull and jawbone near Piltdown in Sussex they believed they had found it. The skull and jawbone were discovered by an amateur archaeologist called Charles Dawson, subjected to various scientific tests and pronounced genuine. The missing link had been found!

The bones of Piltdown Man were believed to be half a million years old, and for 40 years the scientific world never doubted their authenticity. But other finds came to light during this time, some of which made the Piltdown bones seem rather curious; and in the 1950s scientists realised that they could produce teeth very like those of the fossil by filing down the teeth in a chimpanzee's skull. Later, further tests revealed that the jawbone was a fake, and comparatively modern — indeed, it proved to be that of an ape. The skull itself was genuinely much older, and probably that of a human being. In fact, Piltdown Man was an elaborate practical joke. No one ever knew for sure who had perpetrated it — but it was done well enough to fool the scientific world for almost half a century.

IN THE SOUP

Equipment: a tin of soup, tin opener, soup bowls

On a cold winter's day, offer to get some delicious hot soup ready. Go into the kitchen and open a tin of soup, clattering things about as if you were pouring it into a saucepan and heating it up. Take some time over it.

You then appear with the bowls of soup, which you handle carefully, saying they are very hot. You could even blow on one to cool it down. Wait until someone tucks in — and watch the reaction. For the soup is stone cold, you never heated it up at all!

THUMBNAIL TRICK

Equipment: a lighted candle

Hold the lighted candle so that it drips wax on to one of your finger- or thumb-nails. It won't burn you. Let enough drip to coat the nail, and shape it slightly so that it looks like another nail on top of the real one. When you are with a friend, pretend to be picking at your finger-nail, as if it were a nervous habit. Then say, 'Oh dear, I've pulled my nail off!' as you remove the wax 'nail' and hold it out for your friend's inspection.

PENNIES FROM HEAVEN

Equipment: a handful of coins

Lie in wait for a friend, hiding behind a hedge, fence or wall. Then, as the victim approaches, toss a coin into the air so that it lands at his or her feet. Your puzzled friend will stop to pick up the coin, thinking it has fallen out of a hole in the pocket. When he or she walks on again, repeat the trick. You can keep on doing it for as long as the friend looks perplexed and the money lasts. It need not be expensive — ten 1p coins will give you a lot of fun.

You: 'You're very beautiful.'
Friend: 'Thank you. I wish I could say the same about you.'
You: 'You could if you were as big a liar as I am.'

WHAT'S ON THE TELLY?

Equipment: two copies of the *Radio Times* or *TV Times*

If someone you know takes either or both of these magazines you can perform a particularly annoying trick on him. Keep an old copy of the magazine, carefully open the staples and take out the middle pages. When the new issue comes, do the same thing, and replace its middle pages with those of the old one. Fold down the staples again so that the magazine does not appear to have been tampered with. He is going to get a big surprise when Monday or Tuesday evening arrives and he has a strange feeling that he's already seen the programmes he is reading about.

BLOODY FINGER

Equipment: bandage, cotton wool, red paint or ink

If you want to get out of some particularly dreary chore, you could always create a realistic-looking cut finger. Spread blobs of red paint or ink on some cotton wool and on a bandage. First put the cotton wool around your finger, then hold it in place with a piece of bandage. You will have a very nasty-looking bloody finger.

CREEPY-CRAWLIES

Equipment: pipe cleaners, black and green inks or paints

Many people have a horror of big black spiders and caterpillars — particularly in their salad! This, of course, makes them ideal material for practical jokes. Caterpillars can be created by cutting inch-and-a-half lengths off yellow pipe cleaners, and dotting green paint or ink on them. Bend one end slightly to create a head, and there you are. Hide one or two among the lettuce next time you have a salad and you're guaranteed a scream or two.

Pipe cleaners also make wonderful spiders. Take four lengths each of about four inches, and twist them round one another to make eight hairy legs. Paint them black and leave them to dry. Then place them in strategic corners of the room or suspend them on thin thread from lamps, and so on. You can even use the thread to lower a spider on to someone's head, or draw it across the floor towards their feet. Uuuuugggghhhhh!

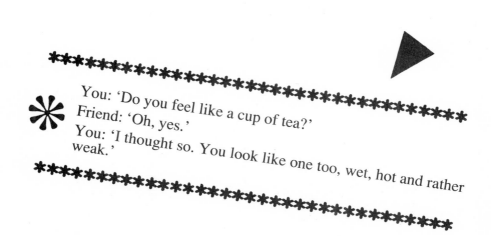

You: 'Do you feel like a cup of tea?'
Friend: 'Oh, yes.'
You: 'I thought so. You look like one too, wet, hot and rather weak.'

UP IN THE AIR

Equipment: a chair, a blindfold, two helpers

This is an amusing trick that goes down well at a party. Choose and blindfold a victim, and ask him to stand on the chair. Place yourself behind it, with your two accomplices standing on each side. Rest your hands on the back of the chair, and get your accomplices to put their hands on the seat.

Now tell your victim that you are going to lift the chair up in the air. You and your accomplices should flex your knees as if you are bending to lift the chair up in the air — but you don't. However, your victim will *feel* as if the chair has been lifted up. You then ask him to jump off the chair. He will be too scared to do so, believing himself to be several feet up in the air. If you are doing this at a party, there will be a great roar of laughter — at which you remove the blindfold, to reveal to the victim that the chair is still on the ground and hasn't moved an inch.

VERY
SILLY
JOKES

For people who
don't mind making
fools of themselves

COMIC DRINK I

Equipment: a comic, a plastic bag or paper cup, sticky tape, some water or lemonade

Say to a friend, 'I have a special magic comic here. I can pour this glass of lemonade into it, and not get wet. Do you believe me?'

Of course, the friend won't. You could even bet your next bottle of lemonade that you can do it; because, naturally, you can. The secret is to attach, by means of sticky tape, a paper cup or polythene bag to the inside of the comic. If you then pour the lemonade carefully, it will go into the cup or bag and not spill all over the place. Make sure, though, that you don't pour in more than the cup or bag will hold.

COMIC DRINK II

Equipment: a plastic bag or paper cup, sticky tape, a drink

This is, in essence, the same trick, but you could cause a great deal of amazement by playing it in public. Fix the plastic bag or cup inside your jacket pocket, or, if you are a girl, inside a handbag. When visiting a café with your friends, wait until someone offers you a soft drink or a cup of coffee. Accept it gratefully, then say, 'It's a bit hot at the moment/I'm not very thirsty just now, I think I'll drink it later.' And you calmly pour the drink into your pocket! Again, take care not to pour in too much.

EAR WIGGLER

Equipment: string, sticky tape

I've never been able to wiggle my ears, though some people can. However, with the mechanism described below, even I can do it. You need two pieces of string, one about 1 foot (30 cm) long, the other about 2 feet (60 cm) long. Tie the longer piece to the centre of the shorter piece, and fix small pieces of sticky tape over each end of the shorter string. Stick the tape, and the string, to the backs of your ears, letting the longer string dangle down your back. Hide it by wearing a sweater or a jacket. Then, by pulling gently on the longer piece of string, you can make your ears wiggle. Try it and see!

GROWLING TUM

Equipment: a piece of cardboard, two rubber bands, two paperclips, a keyring, curtain ring or metal washer

This curious piece of equipment emits a strange growling noise, which, if hidden under your sweater, can sound as if your tummy is letting you know that it is very hungry indeed. Loop the rubber bands round the ring and fold the cardboard in half. Attach one end of each paperclip to the free end of each rubber band, and fix the paperclips to the top and bottom edges of the cardboard as shown in the illustration. Twist the ring and the rubber bands until the bands are taut, and, without letting them unravel again, fold up the cardboard. The device can then be hidden away until required, for example, up your sweater or behind your back. In order to make the growling sound, simply open up the cardboard. The rubber bands will unwind, and the metal ring will vibrate against the cardboard, making a very odd noise indeed.

STICKY SHAKE

Equipment: some jam, honey or marmalade

If you want an extremely silly handshake trick, conceal a spoonful of jam, honey or marmalade in your right hand. When you meet a friend, or have visitors at home, hold out your right hand to shake hands. The victim will have a nasty surprise — and a very sticky hand.

GENUINE JAPES 2

PANORAMA'S SPAGHETTI HARVEST

Panorama, as most people know, is a serious current affairs programme broadcast by BBC Television. In the 1950s it was presented by Richard Dimbleby, a highly-respected broadcaster, and it was on the evening of 1 April 1957 that he introduced an item about Italy's spaghetti harvest.

In the same serious tone as was used for the rest of the programme, Richard Dimbleby described how, in an Alpine region of Italy, the spaghetti was carefully picked from the trees and packed into baskets. 'Many people are puzzled,' he said, 'by the fact that spaghetti is produced in such uniform lengths. But this is the result of many years of patient endeavours by plant breeders, who have succeeded in producing perfect spaghetti.' Film was shown of women carefully picking the long strands, laying it out to dry in the sun, and finally sitting down to a meal of it.

In those days far fewer people travelled abroad for holidays and ate foreign food, and although most people knew spaghetti is produced from dough, many were completely taken in by the programme, and phoned the BBC to ask for further details about the harvest. It was a classic April Fools' Day joke.

WHATTA LOTTA LETTERS!

Equipment: used envelopes

It can take quite a while to prepare this trick, for you need to collect as many envelopes as possible, to open them carefully, and then to stick them down again so that they appear not to have been tampered with. If you feel inclined to take the trouble, you can write or type spoof letters to go inside all the envelopes, but if not, the envelopes themselves will produce quite an effect.

Wait until you have a huge pile of envelopes, then get up first one morning and put them all on the mat, as if the postman has just delivered them. Other people in the house will be amazed at the huge amount of mail that has been delivered.

SNOW MONSTER

Equipment: two buckets and a broomstick

This is a very silly trick to play in the snow. The idea is to fool people into thinking that the Abominable Snowman has walked across the lawn in the night. Get up early and go outside before anyone else is around. Put one foot in each bucket, bend down to take hold of the handles and start walking. Each time you take a step, leaving a huge round footprint, stop to make four little holes in front of it with the stick, so that they look like claw marks. Leave a trail across the lawn, take your feet out of the buckets and return by the path, carrying all the equipment, which you should hide away in a shed. When people come down to breakfast, leave them to discover the monster trail before suggesting it just *might* be the Abominable Snowman.

PINK ELEPHANT Γ

Equipment: none

Say to a friend, 'Ask me if I'm a pink elephant.'

Friend: 'Are you a pink elephant?'

You: 'Yes. Now ask me if I'm a white mouse.'

Friend: 'Are you a white mouse?'

You: 'Of course not, stupid. Didn't I just tell you I was a pink elephant!'

LIQUORICE TRICK

Equipment: a length of black rubber, such as a gasket or piece of draughtproofing

Do you have a friend who likes liquorice? Buy a short piece of black rubber from a hardware shop, and hide it among some genuine liquorice sticks. Pull the false stick so it sticks out of the bag slightly, and offer it to your friend. He or she will accept the rubber 'liquorice' and take a hearty bite — to be sadly disappointed.

WE ARE SIAMESE

Equipment: none

Say to a friend, 'Many years ago, in Siam, there was a society to which only the cleverest people could belong. This society still exists, only it has become very secret nowadays. And since Siam changed its name to Thailand, it has become even more secret than before. I am privileged to be a member of this society.'

Your friend should be very impressed. Then you say, 'I *could* let you join if you would like to.'

Your friend will ask what he or she has to do.

You reply, 'It is all very simple. Close your eyes, spin round six times on one foot, and repeat this ancient Siamese saying six times: OO OO OO WATA NA SIAM!'

RUDE BALLOON

Equipment: a blown-up balloon

Blow up a balloon but don't tie the neck. Instead, let the air out very slowly, and as you do so, pull at the balloon's neck. You will find it makes some very strange noises indeed. Hide the balloon behind your back, and wait for an appropriate moment to surprise people. You'll get some very funny looks!

COMIC CACTUS

Equipment: a pan scourer, a plant pot

The kind of pan scourer that is made of loops of plastic can look remarkably like a cactus if it is placed in a plant pot and packed around with earth. Try giving one as a present to someone. It may take quite a while before it dawns that the cactus is made of plastic.

PILLARBOX PRANK I

Equipment: none

Next time you go to post some letters in a busy street, put your hand inside the slot of the pillar-box and pretend you can't get it out. When someone comes past, pull frantically and ask him or her to help get your hand out. Such efforts will be useless if you curl your fingers round the lip of the slot. The person will go off to get more help — and in the meantime you run off as quickly as you can.

PILLARBOX PRANK II

Equipment: none

As you see a likely victim approaching you pretend that a friend is hidden in the pillar-box and has got stuck in there. With your face held up to the slot, you say things like, 'Don't worry, you'll soon get out. Can you breathe all right in there? Are you getting hungry?' Explain that your friend has got trapped and cannot get out, but that if the kind passer-by will stay and talk to him you will run round the corner and get the postman, whom you have just seen in the distance, to come and unlock the box. Rush to the corner, then, out of sight, turn round to see what is happening. Your poor victim will probably be talking earnestly to the pillar-box, and will look awfully stupid when someone else walks past!

MONKEY BUSINESS

Equipment: a book about monkeys or apes, a small handbag mirror, some Blu-tack

If you don't already have one at home, take out a book about apes or monkeys from your local library. You will also need a small, flat handbag mirror. Put a blob or two of Blu-Tack on the back of the mirror, and attach it lightly to a right-hand page of the book. Take a note of the page number.

Put the book down on the table, and wait until a friend comes in. Say, 'I've got this wonderful book about monkeys. It's got some terrific pictures in it. Look at the one on page so-and-so' (mentioning the page on which you stuck the mirror). Your friend will note the book's title, probably with a picture of monkeys on the cover, and then open the book at the required page — to see himself staring back from the page!

EAR, EAR!

Equipment: some carrots or carrot tops

If anyone ever complains that you don't wash your ears, try playing this trick. Stick some carrot tops (or small carrots if you can't get carrots with tops on) in your ears, and confront the nagger. Say you expect the carrots have grown because you don't always wash your ears very thoroughly, as you have been reminded on so many occasions.

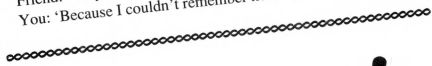

You: 'I was going to get you a box of handkerchiefs for your birthday.'
Friend: 'Why didn't you?'
You: 'Because I couldn't remember how big your nose was.'

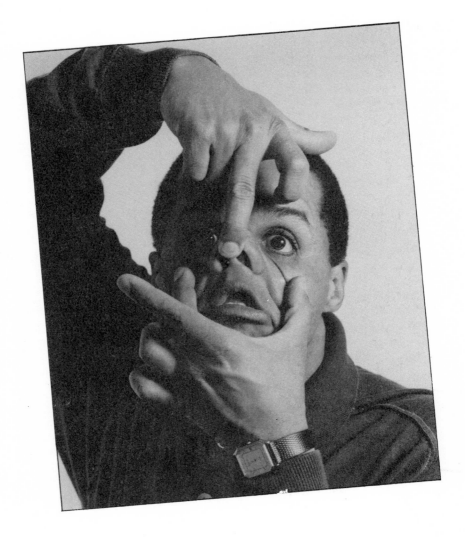

THEATRICAL TRICKS

TRICKS

For those who
like a bit of
play-acting

POP EYES

Equipment: two empty eggshells, black and blue paint, a pin

When you next crack some eggs, slice off the ends with a knife, trying to get a nice, clean edge. Wash out the shells carefully and let them dry. Paint irises and pupils in the centres of the shells, so they look like eyes, and make a pinhole right in the middle so that you can see through them.

Gently put them in place between your eyebrow and your cheekbone, and you will find you can hold them quite easily. If you really want to frighten somebody, put a pair of dark glasses over your eggshell eyes, and then suddenly take them off. Aaaarrrggghhh!

TWO LOVELY BLACK EYES

Equipment: dark blue or grey, plus reddish-coloured eye-shadow

If you can get hold of a range of coloured eye-shadow, you can use it to create two wonderful black eyes. Choose the dark blue or dark grey colours right round the eyes, but if you have access to red or plum-coloured shadow, and possibly yellow, or a little green, use these, too, around the edges. You can then pretend to have been in a terrible fight, or had a spectacular accident, and lap up the kind attention that everyone lavishes on you.

BATTLE SCARS

Equipment: lipstick or red felt-tip pen, some Copydex

If you want to add to your injuries, you can create authentic-looking scars with lipstick or red felt-tip pen and some Copydex. Draw a red line with the lipstick or pen, and then crease the skin on either side. Spread the Copydex over it, and hold the skin in the creased position until the Copydex dries. You will then have a nasty, puckered-looking scar, which should create even more sympathy among your family and friends.

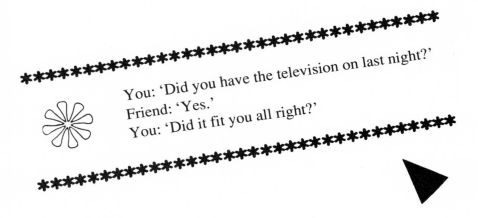

You: 'Did you have the television on last night?'
Friend: 'Yes.'
You: 'Did it fit you all right?'

SMUDGED

Equipment: some dark eye-shadow

Put a little eye-shadow on your index finger and tell a friend that he has a smudge on his face. Offer to remove it, and ask him to hold still while you do so. You then wipe away the non-existent smudge with the finger covered in eye-shadow — leaving a nice smudge on your friend's face.

FISHY BUSINESS

Equipment: a goldfish bowl or fish tank, a carrot, a knife

Cut a slice out of the carrot and work it roughly into the shape and approximate size of a goldfish. Then drop it into the goldfish bowl or tank, alongside the real fish. When someone is on hand to watch, scoop up your carrot fish (take care it's not a real one), shake it about a bit in your hand, so that it appears to be wriggling, and toss it into your mouth. Crunch away at the carrot, remarking that it is rather a bony fish, but tastes very good. What a nasty trick!

GENUINE JAPES 3

THE MAN WHO SOLD THE EIFFEL TOWER

The Eiffel Tower was built for the Paris Exhibition of 1889, and rapidly became one of France's most popular tourist attractions, causing general amazement as one of the tallest structures in the world. But in 1925 an Austrian Count named Victor Lustig and his associate, Daniel Collins, sold it — twice!

The Count invited five wealthy scrap metal merchants to his Paris hotel suite and told them, under a vow of secrecy, that the Tower was in a dangerous condition and would have to be demolished. Secrecy was necessary, he explained, because if the people of Paris found out about it there would be an uproar. He asked the businessmen to put in bids for the scrap metal — about 7,000 tonnes — and the Count accepted the highest, which was from a dealer called André Poisson. At their next meeting M. Poisson gave the Count a cheque for several hundred thousand francs, taking his word that the legal documents would be forwarded within the next few days. But within 24 hours, the Count and Daniel Collins had fled the country.

Surprisingly, André Poisson did not go to the police, probably because he felt so foolish. And because Lustig and Collins realised their trick had worked so well, they returned to Paris and did it again! This time their victim did go to the police, but Lustig and Collins had again fled the country, and were never caught.

CHOPPED-OFF THUMB

Equipment: a thumb-sized carrot, a paper handkerchief or paper napkin, a pair of scissors or a knife

If you keep the carrot for a few days it will begin to go a bit rubbery, and that's when it is ready for using in this trick. Keep the carrot concealed in the palm of your hand, and show your victim the thumb of that hand, so that the carrot can't be seen. Cover your thumb with the paper handkerchief or napkin, and as you do so, push up the carrot so it sticks up in place of the thumb. Ask your friend to feel your 'thumb' — i.e. the carrot; since it is slightly soft it will feel much the same as a thumb through the paper handkerchief. Then suggest that your friend might like to cut off your thumb, or help you to do it. Fascinated, he will probably agree. So get him or her to hold the end of your 'thumb' while you take the scissors or knife and cut off the end, leaving him holding it. Have a chair ready in case he faints!

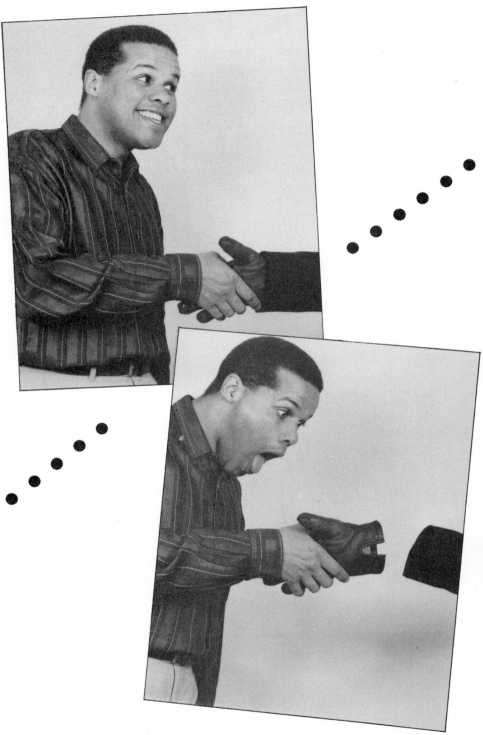

FALLING-OFF HAND

Equipment: a glove, some tissue paper or newspaper

Stuff a right-hand glove with small pieces of newspaper or tissue paper, until it feels quite firm to the touch. Then prepare to give someone a shock. Pull the sleeve of your coat or jacket down over your right hand, and tuck your hand in, just holding the end of the glove with it, so that the glove appears to be your right hand. Wear a glove on your left hand so that nobody wonders why you are wearing only one glove. When you meet a friend, say 'How do you do?' and hold out your right hand. He or she will take it to shake hands, only to find — horror of horrors — that it comes off in his or her hand!

WALKING GHOST

Equipment: an old white dustsheet

If you want to carry the last joke a bit further, dress up as a ghost. All you need is an old dustsheet (make sure it is old and unwanted, because you have to cut holes in it). Put it over your head, work out where your eyes are in relation to the sheet, and cut out two holes so that you can see where you are going. If you cut big holes, so your eyes are visible, you could make yourself look really frightening by outlining them with borrowed eye make-up. Use dark eye-shadow to put rings round your eyes, and perhaps a circle of lipstick, too, so that your eyes are rimmed in red and black. Then you're all set to go haunting. On a summer night you could waft round the garden crying 'Oooooooo', or you could try it indoors late at night. If you have a helper, one of you could work the ghostly piece of paper joke while the other floats around in the sheet. *That* should put the wind up people!

FLUTTERING GHOST

Equipment: a thin sheet of white paper, sticky tape, a long piece of cotton

Here's how to give someone the heebie-jeebies in the middle of the night. Attach one end of the cotton thread to the sheet of paper with sticky tape. Hide the paper in your victim's bedroom out of sight and high up. On top of the wardrobe is an ideal place. Run the cotton, concealed, down behind the wardrobe and along the edge of the carpet, so that it cannot be seen, and out of the door. Carry it through to your vantage point — perhaps the room next door.

Wait until your victim has gone to bed and give him time to settle down and become sleepy. Then start to make some ghostly noises — wail a bit, and moan 'Ooooooooooo' in a creepy sort of way. Now, having set the scene, give a tug on the thread. The paper will waft gently down from the wardrobe towards the poor victim's bed, and he will think it's a ghost. Help!

RASH MOVE

Equipment: a lipstick, or water-soluble red felt-tip pen

Use a water-soluble red felt-tip pen or borrow a lipstick to put spots all over your face and look as if you have measles or chickenpox. Dot them all over your face, and over your chest and tummy, for a realistic effect.

This trick can also be used to horrify people at a swimming pool. Leave your face unspotted, so that you are let into the pool, but before you leave home put the spots on your chest and tummy as before. When you get into your swimming costume, people will start to look very worried. If you intend to play this trick at a pool you had better use lipstick, for the felt-tip pen ink will wash off in the water. But you may find you don't get as far as the water — you are likely to be sent home as a health risk!

LUMPS AND BUMPS

Equipment: a piece of plasticine or Blu-Tack, a bandage or Elastoplast

You can make a realistic-looking lump which you can strap to your hand, arm or even your face with a piece of plasticine or Blu-Tack. Roll it into a ball and strap the bandage or Elastoplast over the top. Strap one to your forehead or nose and say you have walked into a door or lamp-post. Better still, make several and pretend you have been stung by bees or hornets.

QUICKIES

Instant tricks that
can be performed
on the spur of
the moment

COME UP AND SEE ME

Equipment: none

Try this trick on a young friend. Say, 'If I lived up here,' (pointing to his forehead), 'and you lived down here' (pointing to his chin), 'would you come up and see me sometime?' (jabbing him smartly under the nose!)

LOOK OUT!

Equipment: none

This is a great April Fool's joke. It requires no preparation, and takes only a few moments to perform, yet is very effective. Just leap up on to a chair, pointing in horror to a corner of the room, and say 'Look out! There's a great big horrible black spider coming this way! Aaaaarrrrgggghhhh!' Everyone will leap up in horror, and look where you are pointing — to see — nothing. That's the time to shout out, 'April Fool!'

You: 'Dry your hands after you've washed them.'
Friend: 'Why?'
You: 'If you don't, your nails will go rusty.'

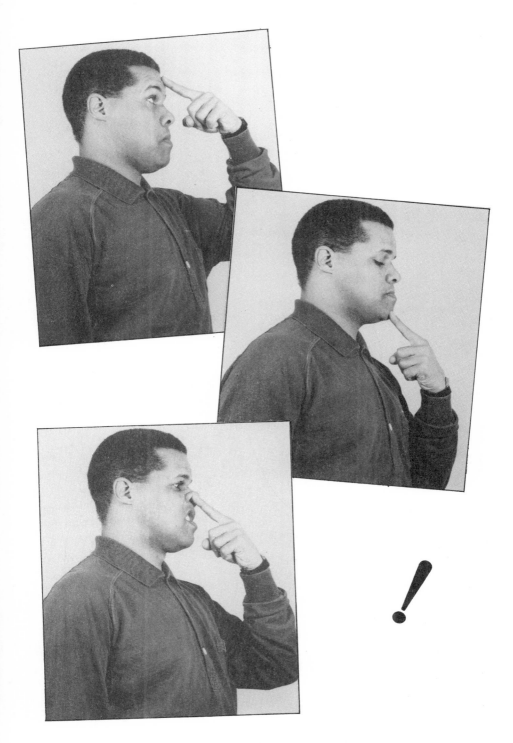

SOLE SEARCHING

Equipment: none

Tell a friend that you know a new way to tell his fortune — a very reliable method that is foolproof. It is based, you say, on the way people wear their shoes. Every pair of shoes has a different pattern of creases and wrinkles created by the individual wearer, and you can tell just by looking at the shoes what kind of person they belong to and so predict what is going to happen to the owner in the near future. If you tell your story well enough, your friend is likely to take off a shoe and offer it eagerly for your attention. Study it carefully, turning it over and examining it in detail. Then say, 'I can see from your shoe that very soon you are going to set off on a long journey.' And throw the shoe as far as you can. A good prediction, eh?

THAT'S TORN IT

Equipment: a scrap of paper

Fold a scrap of paper in half and then tear it into a rough triangular shape. Fold one half of the paper into pleats, leaving the other half unfolded. Then lick the unpleated half, and stick it on to the wall. It will look exactly as if someone has ripped the wallpaper. If you put it at the right height, and stand a chair near it, the effect will be very realistic.

GRIN AND BARE IT

Equipment: none

Say to a friend, 'Imagine you are camping in the Canadian Rockies. You get up in the morning, crawl out of your tent, and walk over to the stream to wash your face. And there in front of you is a great big grizzly bear. There are no trees to climb, and no rocks to hide behind. What would you do?'

Friend: 'Run.'

You: 'What, with a bear behind?'

MIND READING

Equipment: a coin

Ask a friend to take a coin out of his or her pocket or purse and to hold it tightly without letting you see it. Say that by concentrating extremely hard, you will be able to read the date. You stare intently at the clenched fist which contains the coin, frown in concentration, put a hand to your head, and say, 'Yes, I think I'm beginning to see it. The date is . . . erm . . . the date is . . .' and you rattle off today's date! You never actually promised to read the date on the coin!

GENUINE JAPES 4

WELCOME TO SAN SERRIFFE!

Newspapers often publish short items about nonsensical happenings on April Fool's Day, but none can have been taken so seriously as was that in *The Guardian* on 1 April 1977, when it printed a whole supplement about two mythical islands called San Serriffe, whose exact whereabouts were never defined, but which were set somewhere in a tropical ocean. The islands were ruled by a military leader called General Pica, who was pictured in uniform wearing dark glasses, and had a capital city called Bodoni. Long and serious articles, illustrated with photographs, gave details of the islands' economy, their agriculture, their politics, the beginnings of their tourist industry, and other matters, in the same style as is often used for genuine newspaper supplements.

Anyone who has ever had any connection with printing would recognise the terms 'san serif', 'pica' and 'Bodoni', and many readers did, and thoroughly enjoyed the joke. But the newspaper was inundated with requests for further information about the islands from would-be tourists who hoped to discover an unknown tropical paradise, and, as a result, issued car stickers which proudly proclaimed, 'I've been to San Serriffe!'

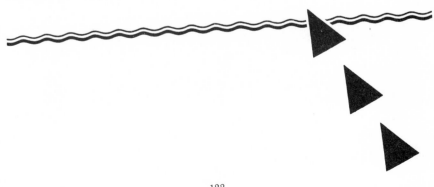

SHORT-DISTANCE TRAVEL

Equipment: none

Next time you have a visitor and see him to the door to say goodbye, remain on the step until he has gone a little way down the road. Then call him back. Wait until he has come all the way back to your gate, then beckon to him confidentially and say, 'How far would you have got if I hadn't called you back?'

This silly trick always seems to work, and it always raises a laugh.

CLICK TRICK

Equipment: a camera

Even if you know nothing about photography, you can have a great time performing this trick. For you don't need a film, just an empty camera. The idea is to pretend to take pictures — and you snap people at their most embarrassing moments. You might, for example, take a picture of your mother or sister with her hair in curlers, of grandad without his false teeth, of your next-door neighbour mowing the lawn in his shorts and displaying his white, hairy legs, of your dad fast asleep in front of the television. You must draw the attention of your models to the fact that you are taking a picture, or the point of the joke is lost. Say, 'Hold it! That's great!' and click away. Your victim will be furious, but you just skip out of the way, saying something about great photography being created from moments like that. Later on, of course, you open the camera to reveal no film inside. April Fool!

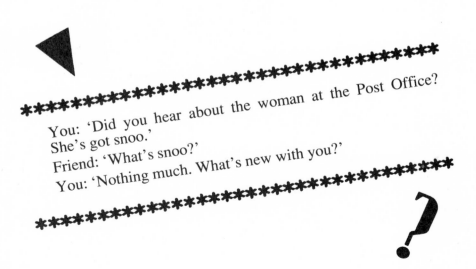

You: 'Did you hear about the woman at the Post Office? She's got snoo.'
Friend: 'What's snoo?'
You: 'Nothing much. What's new with you?'

FIRE DOWN BELOW

Equipment: none

Here's a good quickie which always raises a laugh. Say urgently to a friend, 'Hey! Your shirt tail's on fire!'

He will say worriedly, 'Is it?' and start looking round apprehensively.

You say cheekily, 'It was, but it's out now,' as you whip his shirt tail out of his trousers.

MENTAL ARITHMETIC

Equipment: none

Persuade a friend that you can read his mind. Boast that even if he does a complicated piece of mental arithmetic, you will be able to say the answer.

Ask your friend to think of a number — any number at all. Tell him to double it; then to multiply it by seven; then to add 103; then to take away 57; then to add 500. And finally to take away the number he first thought of.

Remind your friend of your wonderful mind-reading powers, and point out again that you can easily say the answer. Wait until he has got to the end of this marathon of mental arithmetic — and then say just that: 'The answer!'

FINGERS FANDANGLE

Equipment: none

I have eleven fingers. You don't believe me? Well, I can prove it to you. If I start with the little finger of my left hand, as one, the ring finger next to it, as two, the middle finger next to that, as three, and so on, right along my left hand and then all along my right hand, I get ten. Right? Now, if I count backwards, starting with the little finger of my right hand, as ten, the ring finger is nine, the middle finger is eight, the index finger is seven, and the thumb is six. There are five fingers on my left hand, and five added to six makes eleven, doesn't it?

Try this trick on a friend and see if you can convince them.

127

CHEAP EATS

Equipment: 10p

This is a sneaky trick, and not really very nice. But it is clever, and is useful to have up your sleeve if you want to get your own back on someone.

Go to a café with your victim, and just order a cup of tea, or a fruit juice, while he or she orders a hamburger or a delicious pastry. Then say: 'I bet you 10p that I could eat that hamburger/pastry without letting it touch my mouth, lips or teeth.'

Your victim is bound to be intrigued and will let you have a go. Whereupon you start to eat the food heartily. Your companion will protest, 'Hey! That hamburger/pastry is touching your mouth, lips and teeth!'

Mumble, through mouthfuls of food, 'You're right. Looks as if I've lost my bet, doesn't it.' And you hand over your 10p. It's very cheap for a hamburger or a pastry, isn't it?

LOST TENNER

Equipment: none

Try this on April Fool's Day. Say to someone, 'Why did you put that £10 note in the rubbish bin?'

He or she will immediately start to rummage through the bin frantically, and may well end up with its entire contents strewn all over the kitchen floor, looking for the non-existent note. At this stage, say 'April Fool!' — and get out of the way quickly!

ALL TWO MUCH!

Equipment: none

Try this trick on a friend. Say, 'What does TO spell?'
Friend: 'To.'
You: 'And what does TOO spell?'
Friend: 'Too.'
You: 'And what does TWO spell?'
Friend: 'Two.'
You: 'And what is the second day of the week?'
Friend: 'Tuesday.'
You: 'No it isn't. Monday is the second day of the week.'

TIES UP!

Equipment: a victim who is wearing a tie

Ask a friend what a boat does when it goes into harbour. He may give a number of answers, such as: 'Switches off its engine,' 'Drops anchor', 'Puts down a gangplank' and so on, to each of which you say 'no'. Finally he will ask, 'Well, what does it do, then?' To which you reply, 'Ties up!', and as you say it, you get hold of the end of his tie and flick it up into his face.

PHEW!

Equipment: none

Say to a friend, 'If frozen water is iced water, what is frozen ink?'

He or she will reply, 'Iced ink.'

At which you wrinkle your nose, and reply, 'I know you do!'

BABY TALK

Equipment: none

Choose a victim, and show him the palm of your hand. Say that in the very centre of your palm is a tiny, very new baby, and that it is fast asleep. Point to the spot on your palm where the 'baby' is lying, and explain that because it is so tiny and so new, everyone must be extremely careful with it. Then say, touching your palm with each statement:

'Daddy says, "Don't touch the baby."

'Mummy says, "Don't touch the baby."

'Granny says, "Don't touch the baby."

'Grandad says, "Don't touch the baby."

'Auntie says, "Don't touch the baby."

'Uncle says, "Don't touch the baby."

'Sister says, "Don't touch the baby."

'Brother says, "Don't touch the baby."'

Then ask your victim, 'Where is the baby?' He will point to the centre of your palm, whereupon you smack his hand sharply, and say, 'Didn't I tell you — DON'T TOUCH THE BABY!'

MAKING MONEY

Equipment: none

You can fool most people with this trick. Say to someone, 'There's only one way to make money.'

He will say, 'What's that, then?'

At which you reply, cheekily, 'I might have guessed *you* wouldn't know!'

DO COME IN

Equipment: none

Wait until someone in the house is having a bath. Then stand outside, knock loudly on the door, and say, equally loudly, 'Oh, hello, Mrs X (choose the name of a person that would be least welcome in the bathroom at that moment), do come in. My wife/sister/husband/mother would so like to see you.'

The poor bather will sit shivering in the bath, wondering when the unwelcome visitor is likely to burst in through the door.

CROWD STOPPER

Equipment: none

Next time you are with a friend in a crowded street, or on a busy bus or train, give him or her a nudge in the ribs and say, 'Do you realise that you forgot to put on your skirt/trousers before you came out this morning?'

Help! For a moment or two, your friend will be horrified, and if standing in a crowded bus or train, will be unable to look down to see if you are telling the truth or not.

VENTRILOQUISM MADE SIMPLE

Equipment: a dummy, such as a doll, an accomplice

A very simple way of proving what a splendid ventriloquist you are is to have a hidden accomplice who actually does the talking. Before you start giving your performance, hide the accomplice under a table or behind the sofa or the curtains. Sit down on a chair with your dummy, which may be a doll or a teddy bear, or even the family pet (if it doesn't object) and start talking to it. Your accomplice must answer in a funny voice, and you should contort your face a bit, so that you seem to be struggling to throw your voice. You may well fool people for ages.

GENUINE JAPES 5

BUNGA, BUNGA!

In 1910, the flagship of the British Home Fleet was the battleship HMS *Dreadnought*, and many important visitors were received on board and shown around. So when the Commander-in-Chief received a message that the Emperor of Ethiopia and his party would like to visit the ship, it was nothing out of the ordinary.

Little did he know that the 'Emperor' and his party were Cambridge undergraduates in disguise. They included a young man who was to become famous for his practical jokes, Horace de Vere Cole, and Virginia Stephen, who was later renowned as the novelist Virginia Woolf.

The Navy gave them the red carpet treatment throughout, although the students obviously had a problem with the language. One of them was supposed to be the official interpreter, who had to translate the naval Commander-in-Chief's words to the 'Emperor'. He did this by mispronouncing chunks of Latin verse which he knew off by heart, and the 'Ethiopians' expressed their delight at all they saw on board the ship by exclaiming excitedly, 'Bunga, bunga!' The joke was a complete success, and only revealed when de Vere Cole told the story to a newspaper a few weeks later. The Admiralty was full of red faces, but most people enjoyed the joke hugely, and 'bunga, bunga' became a popular catch phrase in the country's music halls.

CATCH A COIN

Equipment: a £1 or 50p coin

Tell a friend that you are going to test his reflexes. Hold up the coin, and ask him to position the thumb and forefinger on either side of the coin, but not actually to touch it, promising that if he catches it when you drop it, he can keep the coin. He will, of course, assume this to be easy — but you are unlikely to lose your money.

Start explaining what you are going to do. Say, 'I am going to drop this coin at any moment, not exactly now, but very soon, and when I drop it you . . .' and drop the coin in mid-sentence. Your victim is most unlikely to have quick enough reflexes to catch the coin before it falls.

If you feel really confident with this trick, you could try it with a £5 note. Hold the note at one end, and again have your victim positioned so that he has to catch it with thumb and forefinger. Someone with really fast reflexes just might manage it, but if you distract him skilfully with your patter, you should be able to prevent him from concentrating hard enough for his reflexes to work at their best.

ANTIDISESTABLISHMENTARIANISM

Equipment: none

Say to a friend, 'Antidisestablishmentarianism is one of the longest words in the dictionary. How many Ts are there in that?'

Your friend will probably say he doesn't know, or may make a guess, such as 'six'.

You reply, 'There are just two — one at the beginning and one at the end — T h a T.'

WHITE FLAG

Equipment: none

A white flag indicates surrender, and that is what this sneaky trick is all about. Say to a friend, 'Would you hit someone after he has surrendered?'

Your friend will, of course, say 'no'. At which point you give him a playful punch, remarking, 'I surrender!'

FIRST AND LAST

Equipment: a peanut or cobnut

Adopting a mysterious tone of voice, say to a friend that you can show him something that has never been seen before by human eyes, and will, after this moment, never be seen again. Your friend will be very puzzled and intrigued.

Then you simply take your peanut or cobnut and remove the shell. The nut inside has never before been seen by human eyes. Pop it into your mouth and eat it. There! It will never be seen again by human eyes. You have done exactly what you said you would do.

NINETY-NINE

Equipment: none

Say to a friend, 'What number comes after ninety-nine?'

Friend: 'One hundred.'

   You: 'And what number comes after nine hundred and ninety-nine?'

   Friend: 'One thousand.'

   You: 'And what number comes after nine thousand and ninety-nine?'

   Friend: 'Ten thousand.'

   You: 'No it doesn't! Nine thousand one hundred comes after nine thousand and ninety-nine. Ten thousand comes after nine thousand nine hundred and ninety-nine!'

If you say this trick quickly enough, you will be bound to catch out your friend.

ELEVEN-LETTER ALPHABET

Equipment: none

Tell someone you can prove that there are only eleven letters in the alphabet. Most people, of course, think there are twenty-six. But, if you write it out like this, you can prove there are only eleven. Look.

T	H	E	A	L	P	H	A	B	E	T
1	2	3	4	5	6	7	8	9	10	11

MAKING YOUR MARK

Equipment: a felt-tip pen, a handkerchief

Ask a friend if you may borrow his handkerchief. (If he doesn't have a real cotton handkerchief, ask for a scarf or a T-shirt). Take it in your hand, and say, 'The trouble with things like this is that they all look exactly the same. Tell you what, I'll make a mark on it with this felt-tip pen so I know it is yours.' And before the horrified eyes of your friend, you draw a thick, black line down the middle of it. At any rate, you appear to do so. Have the felt-tip pen ready with its cap off, hold the handkerchief in the other hand so that your friend can't see the pen, and quickly turn the pen round so that its non-writing end faces the handkerchief. Run this end of the pen down the handkerchief as if you were drawing a black line right down the centre, then quickly turn the pen round again. Your victim will probably grab the handkerchief to see how you have ruined it — only to discover, with surprise, that it is completely unmarked.

SCREAMING AB-DABS

Equipment: none

If you want to give someone a fright, go into a room you know he will be entering shortly and hide in a cupboard, behind a sofa, behind the curtains, under the bed, or wherever you can be sure not to be seen. Then, when you hear your friend enter the room, let out a piercing scream! You will give him the fright of his life!

You: 'Keep your eyes open tomorrow.'
Friend: 'Why?'
You: 'Because you'll bump into something if you don't, that's why.'

THREE QUESTIONS

Equipment: a table and chair

Seat your victim at a table and tell him you are going to ask three questions, each of which may only be answered by a 'yes' or a 'no' given by moving his fingers in a certain way.

Then tell your victim to bring over the thumb of his right hand to meet its little finger (assuming he is right-handed, otherwise he should use the left hand), and keep the fingers in that position while putting the remaining three fingers flat on the edge of a table, as shown in the illustration. The first question must be answered by using the index finger, the second by using the middle finger, and the third by using the ring finger. A 'yes' is indicated by wiggling the finger; a 'no' by lifting the finger off the table. None of the other fingers, or the thumb, must be moved when answering a question. Right. After that lengthy explanation, you are now ready to ask your victim the three questions.

First question: 'Did you have cornflakes for breakfast?' He can answer 'yes' by wiggling the index finger, or 'no' by lifting it off the table.

Second question: 'Are you going away on holiday this year?' He can answer 'yes' or 'no' by doing the same with the middle finger.

Third question: 'Are you a stupid idiot?' The victim will discover that he can only answer 'yes', because it is impossible to lift the ring finger off the table without moving the other fingers!

SILLY MONKEYS

Equipment: none

Say to a friend, 'There were once six very silly monkeys. One day, they were all sitting on a branch of a tree in a row. Their names were Doh, Re, Me, Fah, Soh and Lah. It was a warm day, and they all began to feel very sleepy. And so sleepy did they become, that Doh, Re, Fah, Soh and Lah fell off the branch of the tree. Who was left?'

Your friend will reply, 'Me.'

To which you retort, 'So you're a very silly monkey, are you?'

BOING BOING

Equipment: none

You: 'What is black and goes boing boing?'
Friend: 'A black boing boing?'
You: 'Quite right. And what is red and goes boing boing?'
Friend: 'A red boing boing.'
You: 'What is green and goes boing boing?'
Friend: 'A green boing boing.'
You: 'What is blue and goes boing boing?'
Friend: 'A blue boing boing.'
You: 'What is purple and goes boing boing?'
Friend: 'A purple boing boing.'
You: 'What is brown and goes boing boing?'
Friend: 'A brown boing boing.'
You: 'No, stupid, they don't make them that colour. Don't you know *anything?*'

TWISTED ANKLE

Equipment: none

If you want to get out of doing something, pretend to have twisted your ankle. Limp along (if you can't manage this very well, put a small stone in your shoe and you'll have no trouble) and say how much it hurts. When someone offers to have a look at it, scream with pain when it is touched. With any luck you'll be seated comfortably in front of the fire with a good book and a cup of tea. Of course, this kind of trick can backfire, because you can't very well jump up half an hour later and get on with what you really *do* want to do.

What? Your book didn't have a nice, crisp, new £5 note? Ah well, it is the *Big Book of Practical Jokes!*